HOMECOOKIN'

CLAY GOSS

HOMECOOKIN'

FIVE PLAYS

HOWARD UNIVERSITY PRESS

WASHINGTON, D.C.

1974

Library of Congress Cataloging in Publication Data

Goss, Clay.
    Homecookin': five plays.

    I. Title.
PS3557.078H6   812'.5'4   74-5367
ISBN 0-88258-021-3

ॐ

To my family:

To my mother and my father, Mr. and Mrs. Douglas Jackson;
To my brother, Conway;
To my wife and children—Linda, Iisha, and Uhuru.

ॐ

Contents

HOMECOOKIN'

OurSides

CHARACTERS 🦈

MAN, *middle-aged*
WOMAN, *middle-aged*
CROWD, *various types of Black people going to work*
> MAN *and* WOMAN *represent every black man and every black woman in their neighborhood. They represent each and every experience as well. Therefore, each sentence and line that they recite should build whatever characterization they are attempting to reach together — that recognizability, that mutual understanding that they, the community and its experience and history will one day be forced to resolve. Whatever each character says to the other one is an insight into the next line that is spoken. It is as if the characters are taking a survey of all their lives and placing them into a perspective.*
> *"Who are these people?" — that is the question the man and woman should be driven to answer. For in their desire to get together, the audience (as many members of both sexes in the audience as possible) should see a glimpse of themselves or their past or a part of their experience. They should sell all of our sides.*

SETTING 🦈

Early morning. MAN *and* WOMAN *enroute to work.* MAN *is wearing gray working clothes, lunch pail in hand, folded newspaper tucked under his arms.* WOMAN *is wearing plain cotton dress and three-quarter length jacket. A bulging pocketbook hangs from her shoulder. She is holding on tightly to a flowered plastic shopping bag, an umbrella hanging from it. A sweater is in her hand. Sign on walls says Columbia Avenue Station.* MAN *is standing on stage left.* WOMAN *is standing stage right with* CROWD *between them. They are far apart looking away from the other one. They come together as play goes on. Until ending of the crowd scene, they act as if they are being jostled by some imaginary rowdy morning crowd. Both are pissed off about being jostled.*

MAN and WOMAN face the audience as they recite their dialogue. As the play progresses and they get to know each other more they begin to stare, talk and size up an imaginary figure in the audience. Then they might begin to glance in each other's direction. More and deeper looks as the play progresses until the last lines of the play where the characters, through what they had spoken and realized, have consciously and dramatically turned their bodies and soul inward in each other's direction.

MAN

The people I knew, the people I still know of, picked boogies out of their noses and coolly smeared them on the side of their trousers with not an inch of embarrassment showing on their faces.

WOMAN

And after they spoke, after they finished saying what they had to say, the day that it was would go on being that day. Tomorrow would be the next day and so on and so on and so on and so on and—

MAN

So on weekdays me and the people I knew, the people I still know of, would walk on up to Broad Street at Columbia and catch a subway to work. We never spoke, 'cause we knew we were neighbors.

WOMAN

Women would be there fixing their makeup or adjusting their girdles so the edges wouldn't show through their dresses, you know what I mean.

MAN

The men would be blowing their noses with bright-colored snot rags they had received on Christmas day. Or they would be fidgeting with their muscular hands like they was about to strangle somebody. Some would just stare off across the subway tracks to the crowd on the other side.

WOMAN

Fascinated by the no spitting sign in red and white on the green-and-blue tile wall.

MAN

Naw baby, it was red and white tile, the sign was green and blue. Don't you remember?

WOMAN

Who are you, huh? Just who are you?

MAN

Your old neighbor. The lunatic up the street who beat his wife on weekends. Who worked down out the Richmond Sugar plant near the dock. Say, didn't you work at Campbell Soup?

WOMAN

Yeah, how did you know? I only worked part-time.

MAN

Yeah, I know, during the tomato season, like my wife did. That's how I got you confused. I really dug tomato soup. Was it fun?

WOMAN

Was it fun?

MAN

Yeah, working at the soup plant with my wife.

WOMAN

I . . . I don't really remember your wife, but I do remember the old neighborhood.

MAN

Was it fun, huh—all them red tomatoes—did it make you think of Italy?

WOMAN

Italy! Your wife must've told you about the supervisors. The lady who worked next to me was from Puerto Rico. Didn't speak no English or nothin'. All she said was *mawee gracius* and do.

MAN

I think I hear the train, or was that my life?

WOMAN

I think it was your life, 'cause it's a few minutes late. The train was always on time. You sure you from the old neighborhood? What was my old man's name—one, two, three, four—

MAN

What you countin' for?

WOMAN

I'm given you till ten to tell me Brady's name—five, six, seven, eight, nine.

MAN

His name was Brady, use to write numbers down at the factory.

WOMAN

Shhhh, not so loud, that wasn't my husband. But it was close enough. You've changed since then.

6

MAN

I talk out now sometimes.

WOMAN

Weren't you one of the families whose son got in trouble?

MAN

Both of 'em at the same time, too—armed robbery—ten to fifteen years.

WOMAN

My Brady got life. Somebody ratted on 'em. [looks suspiciously at MAN]

MAN

Don't look at me, woman. Back then I didn't see or hear nothin'. All I did was wait for the subway to go to work and to come back home.

WOMAN

When you got there was everything O.K.? I mean—

MAN

Well, the police said it was pure murder. Plus she had been sexually assaulted several times.

WOMAN

Raped, huh. Your old lady got raped, huh—goddam! My Brady got strangled in prison. Some dude he shortchanged a couple of years back. Ran in to 'em again in the prison. I can see that dude now, on top of old Brady with his gangster hands around his throat saying—

MAN

[with hands around an imaginary throat] Motherfucker, remember me! Do you remember me from the last time? You remember my face?

WOMAN

Or what race I was, what race I was in, what race I saw every

7

morning waiting on the subway, going nowhere going no . . . no place but still in a . . . in a race with space.

MAN

There wasn't much space. I'd shine my shoes. A habit I couldn't break, you know. By the time I got to work they'd be all scuffed up. The crowds, you know. All them people.

WOMAN

I was one of 'em. So was you. But we was quiet then. Pissed off but silent every morning.

MAN

Night before she died I had really kicked her ass. Kicked it good, too. Really kicked her ass. Still ain't sorry 'bout that.

WOMAN

Brady never touched me. Never touched me even at night when we was alone. He was always runnin', always hustlin' for some cash.

MAN

I bumped into you once one mornin' as we was getting on the train.

WOMAN

Did you say "Pardon me?"

MAN

Yeah, you remember then.

WOMAN

'Cause you said "Pardon me." All I was expectin' was " 'Scuse me" or just a glance, you know. But you were the one who said "Pardon me."

MAN and WOMAN

Pardon me.

8

MAN

That morning I really had kicked her ass. She said she was gonna leave me. Go away.

WOMAN

I know Brady wasn't no good. We didn't have no kids but I could've never left him. Cause wit' us it was different.

MAN

Pardon me.

WOMAN

Stop saying that, mister, you're making me blush. Now, stop saying that. You hear me now, stop saying that. You hear me now?

MAN

I want to stop saying it, but does it really mean that much to you, lady? Two little words, I mean. Just a simple saying like "Pardon me."

WOMAN

Please, mister.

MAN

[*pleadingly*] Pardon me.

WOMAN

Mister, I said please, mister.

MAN

Pardon me. [*More lovingly and pleading over and over at timed intervals, as* WOMAN *talks on about her life, the* MAN *says "Pardon me" every conceivable soul way with every conceivable gesture with his body.*] Pardon me, pardon me.

WOMAN

When I'd wake up in the morning, Brady would be laying there beside me with sticky sleep all in his half-open eyes. He'd be snoring. Always caught up in snoring. Sometimes he'd be breaking wind real loud like. He wouldn't be doing it to be rude, you know. To be cruel or nothin'. That was just Brady breaking wind in his sleep and powerin' hisself to another adventure. My Brady like TV westerns. My Brady loved to watch the westerns on TV, and then there were the fights, the boxing matches every Wednesday and Friday with the shaving-blade commercials with Willie Mays or Hank Aaron with foamy white lather all over their face talking 'bout a "cool clean shave and do." Brady had so many of them razors. Lord, he had so many different types of razors: steel-edge, chromium-blade, injector, dijector; God, he had so many razors and combs, good Lord, Brady had his share of combs. All different kinds of hair pomade that he put on before he went to bed. He was always stealing my stockings for caps, and every morning his head would be a dark shiny street of Nat-King-Cole-styled waves for days. I'd cook his breakfast when I had time, then leave. Walk on up to the subway to go to work. I'd come back home from work on the subway. And when I'd get off the train I'd go through the exit bars and up to the steps, to the street, and start walking and walking and walking and walking. [*says "walking" every conceivable way as* MAN *is speaking.*]

MAN

She said that our thing was over. That she was gonna leave the next day while I was at work. Threw a glass at me, two glasses. Wouldn't even clean 'em up, just left 'em there all cracked up in pieces of glass chips caught up in the rug. I caught her by the shoulder from behind and smacked her face good, you hear. I didn't wanta do it, you understand, but she, well I had to hit her 'cause she wouldn't listen to me anymore. Blamed me for what happened to the boys. Put all the blame on me as if she hadn't been around. Like I led 'em to stealing or something. Can you imagine that, me leading 'em to armed robbery. Hit her good across the face. Then I told her about how we use to be happy when we was living down in Tallahassee. How we use to go for them walks every Thursday evening. Check out the show over at the Strand or the Liberty whenever a new movie came in. You know, before we came up here to the city, to this neighborhood with row-to-row houses and dog shit scattered lazily on every other sidewalk square. She said that our thing was through, over, and that that was that. Next day she was gone—dead—I had to kick her ass.

WOMAN

Pardon me!

MAN

For what, asking information? What's it to me, anyway? What's it to you, lady?

WOMAN

Just . . . just that we bumped our sides one rainy morning.

MAN

Was it raining, too?

WOMAN

We bumped our sides one raining morning and you said "Pardon me" instead of just walking away. Then you were gone.

MAN

I was kinda late for work. Late for the job. Gotta punch in before I start. [laughs to himself] Yeah, have to punch in before I begin.

WOMAN

To understand, mister. To . . . to understand!

[CROWD is starting to appear, pushing and shoving as people do when waiting for the morning subway. CROWD gets in between the MAN and WOMAN, making noises, laughing, coughing, spitting up phlegm. The MAN and WOMAN still try to talk while being pushed apart.]

11

MAN

To understand what, lady? What was there to understand?

WOMAN

What was happening? What was going on in the neighborhood?

MAN

What was going on? What was going on was what was going on. What else could have been going on?

WOMAN

You . . . you could have won.

MAN

Whaaaat? Won what! Who are you, anyhow? Where's the train for Christ sake.

WOMAN

You could have won. We could have won. We touched our sides and you said "Pardon me" and I *did.*

MAN

Did what? You *did* what?

WOMAN

I accepted what you had to say—we could have made it the very next day if we had tried.

MAN

But I was still a little sleepy. Still half asleep sorta, sorta in a daze the crowd was pushin' so, actin' rowdy. [*to one of* CROWD] Get your elbow out my back, buddy. Stop pushing back there, dammit!

WOMAN

I heard you hollering, screamin' and hollering, trying to stay alive along with me.

MAN

They pushed me into you, I think. I think they pushed me into you. That's why I didn't catch the meaning. 'Cause I didn't bump into you on purpose.

[*sound of train coming*]

WOMAN

But it was on purpose. It had to be on purpose. We was living in that run-down neighborhood on purpose. Together for once on purpose. Together for once on time.

[CROWD *still rowdy*]

MAN

With a purpose.

[*They look at each other, struggle to get closer while* CROWD *pushes them far apart. They extend arms till they grab hands.*]

WOMAN

With a common purpose. To go on.

MAN

And on.

WOMAN

And on.

MAN

And on.

MAN and WOMAN

And on.

[CROWD *scrambles forward, then runs offstage.* MAN *and* WOMAN *hold hands over their heads in triumph, then embrace.*]

Lights dim out
End

Homecookin'

CHARACTERS 🎵

ROBERT, *average height, brown-skinned male with young-boy (Marvin Gaye-ish) face. He is dressed in a marine uniform —rank sergeant.*

CLAY, *tall, dark-brown-skinned male with noticeable moustache. He has an Afro hair style (not too long). His manner and dress are those of a college student from a black university that could have had student uprisings against the administration. He wears conservative, pale-colored daishiki and corduroy pants. He is home on vacation and coming back from a party on the other side of town.*

HOMOSEXUAL, *queen figure, dressed half as woman, half as man; modish fashions. He has a huge Afro hair style with an effeminate leopard-cloth daishiki. He is light-skinned and tall. More faggoty than the most obvious faggot. He has two large suitcases that are full of clothes worn by the different characters he will play.*

SETTING 🎵

Opening scene finds CLAY *sitting in a subway seat, legs crossed, and looking around indiscriminately, at no one in particular. Every now and then he will make movements as if he is biting his fingernails; also, he looks at his watch as if he is behind some imaginary schedule. Occasionally he yawns noticeably, exaggerating with his arm spread. Lights flicker on and off, giving the illusion of motion, fast and furious motion. Also, stations (if possible) flash by.* CLAY

17

*has an empty seat beside him. The door of the train is to
his left. There are more seats in a row up against windows
to the left of the door. All seat space in train is taken up by
large cardboard images of people—black, white, Puerto
Rican, policeman—except two: the one space beside* CLAY,
*and one space among the cardboard characters sitting to
the left of the door.*

*During play, noise (common subway noises) can be heard.
Actors react to it as if annoyed. After a time, the train
pulls to a stop. Doors open. In walks the* HOMOSEXUAL,
who looks to his right at CLAY, *takes seat among cardboard characters at left.* ROBERT *walks in just before
doors shut. Lights flicker fast again (motion-sound).* ROBERT
*stumbles, giving the appearance of being a little high. He
looks left and right a couple of times and then sits beside*
CLAY. CLAY *looks at him, especially at his sergeant stripes,
then continues looking forward.* ROBERT *looks at* CLAY, *then
does about four exaggerated double takes and taps* CLAY *on
the shoulder heavy-handedly.* CLAY, *looking annoyed, looks
his way.*

ROBERT
Hey man! 'Member me? 'Member me? H. J. Widener School.
Thirteenth and Thompson. 'Member me, Robert, your best
friend in the third grade and all of that shit?

[CLAY *looks at him, trying to recognize the marine.*]

Aw, come on, man, I know you know who I am. 'Member
H. J. Widener School, Mr. Goodheart's class? I know you do,
man. Shit, I know you do.

CLAY
[*kind of confused*] Mr. Goodheart . . . H. J. Widener . . .
H. J. . . . yeah . . . yeah . . . yeah, yeah . . . Robert . . .

18

Robert—what's happening, brother? Damn, I thought I would never see your skinny ass again. [*rears back, happy as hell, laughing*] Yeah! H. J. Widener School, Thirteenth and Thompson, with the square across the street with the concrete basketball courts. *Kiss my motherfuckin' ass!* I'd almost forgotten I'd gone there up till the fourth grade. Up until I moved from down the way up to Germantown. Yeah . . . [*reflectively*] What's happenin' with you, man? What you been doing?

ROBERT

[*smiling*] What's it look like I been doing? Being messed over, that's what. I been in the marines now 'bout . . . [*counting his fingers*] three and a half years. Hell, I just got back from the Nam about two weeks ago. But, look, I don't want to talk 'bout that, at least not right now, 'cause we both got a long ways to go on this subway. I'm up in Germantown, too. Staying with my mom. [*Coughs violently.*]

[CLAY *just looks at him.*]

Remember the square, man? 'Member the basketball games, the gangs, the bitches, the neighborhood heroes?

CLAY

Yeah, brother, [*smiling*] I remember all that shit. I even remember light, bright Loretta Clarke. Nine years old with titties, man. [*makes expressions with his hand over his chest*] Big titties, jack. Bosoms, they were so large.

ROBERT

[*laughing*] You know I 'member her, man. She dug you and me 'cause we was the smartest cats in the room. Me and you the smartest [*laughs louder*] cats in the room. Man, do you 'member Mr. Goodheart?

[*At this mention of Mr. Goodheart's name, the* HOMO-SEXUAL *opens one of his suitcases, pulls out a sports jacket*

19

and horn-rim glasses, puts them on, along with a bow tie (clip on) —then pulls out a ruler and two textbooks.]

Mr. Goodheart, that white motherfucker who taught at H. J. Widener. Do you remember that cat, man? . . . Clay . . . That's your name, Clay . . . ?

CLAY
Yeah, bro', I remember Mr. Goodheart. He was O.K. I guess he was all right.

ROBERT
Man, Mr. Goodheart, he knew what was happenin', jack. He knew there was no future for most of the black cats in that school. But he was such a nice cat. Such an idealistic motherfucker that he couldn't tell us. He couldn't come out then and say, "Look here, yawl. There ain't really gonna be no future in this country for you people. Like forget about college and real success . . . real, *real* success, [*laughs*] 'cause you ain't gon' really see it." Naw, he couldn't tell us that, so he just kept on talking 'bout college in hopes that maybe *one* of us would make it.

[During ROBERT's *dialogue, the* HOMOSEXUAL *has risen from his seat and taken a place directly in front of* CLAY. *He is facing sideways, looking back toward his seat. Soft, weird flute music plays. Stage lights dim with pastel coloring.]*

HOMOSEXUAL
Clayton . . . [*louder*] Clayton . . . [*louder*] Clayton . . . Answer me, boy. Clayton?

CLAY
[*boyish*] Yeyeye . . . yes, Mr. Goodheart. Are you calling me?

HOMOSEXUAL
[*smiling*] You know I'm calling you, Clayton. I've been trying

20

to speak with you alone, all day. Now . . . now . . . let me have a word with you before you go home. It's O.K. with you?

CLAY
[*boyishly*] I guess so, Mr. Goodheart. Robert's waiting over at the square to play some basketball . . . I guess so, Mr. Goodheart.

HOMOSEXUAL
Relax, Clayton. [*turns and faces* CLAY, *ignoring* ROBERT *as if he's not there. Indeed he is not.*] I'm not going to keep you long. You see, I've been informed that you won't be with us at Widener next fall. Seems as if you're moving away to Germantown. Is that so, Clayton?

CLAY
Yes it is, Mr. Goodheart.

HOMOSEXUAL
Well, you're a lucky child, Clayton. Very lucky, indeed. Very lucky, indeed, to have the opportunity to get away from Widener School, Clayton. To get away from North Philadelphia and all of its negative elements: the crime, the filth, the nig . . . [*corrects himself*] the people with their uneducated ways. You're a very lucky boy, indeed.

CLAY
I guess so, Mr. Goodheart. I kinda wish I didn't have to go.

[HOMOSEXUAL *shows annoyance.*]

You know, all of my pals and all. Especially Robert, 'cause he's my best buddy. Momma tells me that I'll have to adjust and get new friends. She says I'll probably never see Robert again for a long, long time. Maybe even never.

HOMOSEXUAL
Humph! Robert. Well, Robert isn't as fortunate as you, Clay-

ton. He'll take care of himself in time. You just be happy that you're getting a chance to better yourself. Don't worry about the Roberts, Clayton. Just better yourself and use your opportunity to get eventually in college so you can get away from poverty and [*hesitates, looking at* ROBERT] . . . and ignorance. Do you hear me, Clayton?

CLAY

Yes, Mr. Goodheart.

HOMOSEXUAL

And you forget about that Robert, do you hear!

CLAY

Yes, Mr. Goodheart. Yeah!

HOMOSEXUAL

Clayton, it's not that I don't like Robert. Why, he's an excellent student. It's just that you have an opportunity, a glorious opportunity that makes you different. Makes you better. Do you understand that, Clayton?

CLAY

Yes, I understand [*turning his head away, looking at* ROBERT] . . . yes, I understand, Mr. Goodheart.

[HOMOSEXUAL *walks back quickly, freakishly, to seat. Takes off costume, puts it back in suitcase. Light flashes back on. Motion. Motion. Subway scene once again.* HOMOSEXUAL *puts on a jacket, Brook's Brothers type.*]

ROBERT

Man, you had it a little better than the rest of us. You and your older cousin. What was his name again?

CLAY

Bill.

ROBERT

Yeah, that's right, Bill. Your mom was a teacher and all. You had it better. A little better. But there was something different about you than your cousin, man. And that's why I'm glad as hell to run into you now that we are grown men.

[HOMOSEXUAL *rises, looking at* ROBERT *and* CLAY *from in front of his seat.*]

Man . . . your cousin is a faggot.

[CLAY *looks at* ROBERT, *shocked.*]

He's a punk. He's a rotten-ass motherfucking punk. He's a—

CLAY

What you talkin' about, Robert? What are you talkin'—

ROBERT

[*loudly interrupts*] He's a punk, man. Shit, we're grown men, so I'm not gonna lie. If you don't dig what I'm saying 'bout your kin, then we can fight right here on the subway. Fuck it. But I'm not saying all this in a bad way. I'm just telling you 'cause I think it's important. Your cousin is a punk, man. I saw the cat downtown on Market Street when I first got home on leave.

[*Lights dim on* ROBERT *and* CLAY; *lights come up dreamily on* HOMOSEXUAL.]

So I walked up to him and said, What's happenin', brother, 'member me, H. J. Widener?

HOMOSEXUAL

No, I don't remember you or H. J. Widener.

[ROBERT *and* CLAY *look at* HOMOSEXUAL.]

23

ROBERT

And the cat looked at me strange, man. Looked down at me strange, man.

CLAY

Robert, maybe he didn't recognize you, brother, it's been kinda long, you know . . .

HOMOSEXUAL

[*loudly*] I recognized the motherfucker. You know I did, Sonny. But why should I speak to him? The lowlife nigger motherfucker. I didn't spend my whole life gettin' good grades to keep remembering cats like Robert and schools like H. J. Widener.

ROBERT

Well, I didn't mind that, 'cause I was just so happy to see someone from the old neighborhood. I said to him, "Look here, let's go into Horn and Hardart's if you're not too busy. I'll buy the lunch."

HOMOSEXUAL

Oh, yeah—well I'm busy. That's why I got on this kinda suit and you got on that uniform. 'Cause I'm busy making more money so I can be out there instead of in there or over there in Vietnam.

ROBERT

Man, I just wanted to look at the cat. Talk to him. Reminisce maybe a little with him.

HOMOSEXUAL

Reminisce about what? The time you beat me in the four forty over at the square? Embarrassing me in front of Sonny, huh. Or do you want to talk about getting good marks and graduating number one in your class or going to college, a white college, not no nigger college down south. A white college, and graduating on a warm summer morning in June with no time to reminisce 'bout nothing except yourself, who got you where you was at. Now how are we going to reminisce when we was never we?

ROBERT

The cat overed me, man. Just kept on gettin' up. Didn't even look back.

CLAY

Bro', I'm sorry about that, really.

[HOMOSEXUAL *sits back down, takes off apparel.*]

ROBERT

Ain't no use in you being sorry. 'Cause you didn't do nothin', never did, Clay. You was never like that, even though you had an opportunity, too. You might have been like him but you never showed it. You in college, Clay? Where do you go?

CLAY

Yeah, Robert. I'm in college. I go to Howard down in D.C.

ROBERT

Solid, down there with all them beautiful black biddies with them soft thighs. Well, I'm gonna tell you somethin', Clay. And if I stutter forgive me, man. [*coughs violently again*] I digs me some Scotch on the rocks with a little grass to make it gas. [*laughs loudly*] You see, man, I can tell that somewhere . . . somehow, somewhere, you done seen the light. The light that says there ain't no real future for black folks in this country. Though you probably got a good summer job and know maybe some very smart people—you still know that there ain't no real future for you or me and that's why we always was, *is*, will be, *is be* [*laughs*] brothers. Soul brothers. Brothers right down in the souls where only our consciences [*laughs*] know for sure. And we sho' is sure.

[CLAY *is nodding his head in agreement while* HOMOSEXUAL *puts on black graduation cap and stands up.*]

25

CLAY

I can dig where you're comin' from, Robert . . . yeah! Yeah!
. . . Brother.

[*They do the black handshake and grin.*]

ROBERT

Man, we grown men now. True men now. Look at me, Clayton.
[*slurring his words as alcohol is taking its toll*] Look at me. I'm
a man. I ain't accepted, I ain't cared about, I ain't even seen.
But still I'm a man.

CLAY

A hell of a man, brother.

ROBERT

Not a man like some half-dick cat like your cousin, who is considered a man in this punk-ass society. But a man. A man 'cause
at an early age I realized there was no real future. You know,
like *no* as in *zero* future. Like I still want to be able to make it
and all that but I know there ain't no real future while I'm
some damn slave, dammit . . . shit. [*laughs*] . . . Naw, man,
ain't no future, Clay. Just dreams to hold on to for the moment.
Remember that song, "This Magic Moment"? It took me by
surprise.

[*They both laugh and slap hands.*]

Man, am I fucked up tonight! That Scotch leaps out walls.
Man, what you do in college, Clay?

CLAY

I'm in pre-law, Robert, but what I like doin' is writin' plays and
poems—you know, black shit like LeRoi Jones and Don L. Lee.

ROBERT

Yeah, I heard of them dudes. 'Specially that Jones . . . crazy motherfucker, but he's *mean*. I like it when he say—"Up against the wall, motherfucker,

[*joined in by* CLAY]

this is a stick-up."

[*They crack up laughing. Lights stop flashing—no motion.*]

HOMOSEXUAL
Black student 303020 raise your hand.

[CLAY *raises his hand.*]

Black student, you have handed in the worst poem I have ever read in my life. What in the blazes could you have been thinking about?

CLAY
Somethin' you don't know anything about, Professor Heartgood.

HOMOSEXUAL
And what might that be, Mister 3-0-3-0-2-0?

CLAY
[*manly*] Black folks, Professor Heartgood. The black thoughts of a black folk called *me sincerely*.

HOMOSEXUAL
You sincerely, Mister 3-0-3-0-2-0. *You, sincerely* have received an F in creative writing for this piece of . . . this piece of trash. [*walks over to* CLAY, *hands him the paper*] Now you sincerely read this F paper to the class so they can hear some black [*laughs*] thoughts.

[CLAY *reads his poem, "And if I Wake Before I Die," to*

27

ROBERT *and* ROBERT *nods yes and vocalizes "yes" and "yeah, man," throughout the poem, gradually getting excited and loud.*]

CLAY

Late at night I have heard the
    heat come on
        and go off into my
    dreams to warm me
        cold and hot
    together sometimes I have
        felt the stars shine through
the blinds and breathe the chilly
        blue air sneaking through
          the storm-glass windows
        warm hot together sometimes
        pyramids enter my mind
          becoming me and all my
        friends dressed in Arab clothing
          snorting cocaine in a
          back room apartment building
        Roman soldiers stinging my back
        with whips shouting at me to
          stop daydreaming and pick up
          another stone
        Zulus piercing their ears
While Nubian women masturbate
    secretly in their huts
        children being born bleeding
    passages from the Bible called
        "Fairy Tales For Pious Faggots"
    who insert corks up their rubberized
    assholes praying for a fart
    warm hot together sometimes
    candles sing and whisper memories

of my grandfather drunk on Saturdays
        straight on Sundays holding my
hand on a bus heading for Bethle-Ham
and potato-salad cabarets
The preacher's wife fell out and died
        of a stroke and
        The Whole Congregation Cried
        The Whole Congregation Cried
                making analogies in their minds on
                how the Christman must have tried
                and failed and spoke and was jailed
                like Martin King a couple of years
                before the sanitation workers' strike
                        warm hot together sometimes
        like a rooster who pees with an
                aluminum dick made in Tennessee
                Forgetting to Crow in the Morning
                Forgetting to Crow in the Morning
                Forgetting to Crow in the Morning
        letting everyone on the farm sleep an
        hour late
                milk turning to butter right there
                in the cows' five titties
                        While the Cup ran away with the
                                                Spoon
                        While the Cup ran away with the
                                                Spoon
                        of methedrine gold dust
                        white as snow and eighteen inches deep
                        forty days you'll get no sleep
                        forty days you'll get no sleep
        and drop alive at the end of the week
        praying to a junkie for more warm hot
        together sometimes messages from
        the mediator sun who rises an

hour later in the west yawning
and tired himself of
The Way Things have been Going
The Way Things have been Going
He don't want to shine
He don't want to shine and
make people Blacker and Sadder and
Blacker and Madder and
Blacker and Badder and
Blacker and Blacker and Blacker
poor rich together sometimes
warm hot together sometimes
dead alive together people
staying awake at night wondering
about the twelve o'clock-lunch-break
whistle
Will it Ever Break
Will it Ever Break for
God's sake will it ever become an
antiquated fossil found by some
future archaeologist named
Songhay or Mali or Ghana
Dick Gregory laughing at you or
Dick Gregory laughing at you performing
for him in the concentration-camp
ovens it's so hot brothers like
Africa used to be before *they* took
us away   before *they* took
us away and told *us* to go to sleep
Tomorrow was the new world
with old houses for the talented tenth
and project dungeons for the lower rents
warm hot together sometimes happy
dead alive together sometimes sad
Hoping that Rooster won't Fuck up Again

Hoping that Rooster won't Fuck up Again
        For God's sake brothers
            don't mess up again
        like the house-trained niggers
    who turned in Denmark Vesey
        or the warm hot blood that
        oozed out of Bessie
            Didn't she sing the Blues Yawl
            Didn't she sing the Blues Yawl
    weren't you proud of that fat black
    sister who sang with all her heart
    until she died
            Didn't You Cry Brothers
            Didn't You Cry Brothers
and go to bed with honky thoughts in your
heads
        evil thoughts in your heads
            turning over and over till
            Dinah came on the scene and
    ain't Aretha mean as anything
    with a truthful mouth singing
        warm hot sometimes dead alive
    soul songs played on bargain-store stereos
        loud and clear like the forgotten tear
        of Emmett Till's mother
        hoping that rooster *will* fuck up *again*
        and give you and me and all of *us time*
Just a little time to get *our* thing together and rise up
Warm Hot Together Sometimes one unsuspecting
        morning like the sun
                        Amen.

[ROBERT *claps and laughs admiringly at poem's end.* HOMO-
SEXUAL *frowns, flicking his wrist at* CLAY *and pursing his
lips, making a sound.*]

HOMOSEXUAL
[*loudly with finality*] An F, 3-0-3-0-2-0.

CLAY

I don't care, Professor Heartgood. I listened to you before and it got me no place. Fuck you, you 4-F motherfucker. The only poems you like are by white poets and you just mad 'cause you can't be their girl. The class dug the poem and that's all I care about. So, fuck you.

HOMOSEXUAL

My Lord, 3-0-3-0-2-0. I just give up on you.

CLAY

Thank you and good night.

[HOMOSEXUAL *takes off his hat and returns to his seat. Lights flicker again—motion.*]

ROBERT

Man, a lot of the cats from the old neighborhood, they got killed over in the Nam. It seemed to me like God [*smiles reflectively, as when he might have been into religion*] had said, [*talking like God*] "O.K., you guys, I've given you your chance to fight . . . 'get some ass' . . . and become a man. I'm sure you all—yawl—realize now that there is no real future for any of you." [*pointing arms like shooting an M-14 rifle*] Bim Bam Death. [*smiles sarcastically, then continues after a short pause*] . . . Talking 'bout death, man, that's another thing that's gettin' me down . . . being a sergeant and all . . . you know.

CLAY

No, I don't know, Robert. What do you mean?

ROBERT

Well . . . when I was over in the Nam I had to send out

patrols on missions. Man, I had to tell those . . . those doomed cats what to do, where to go, and all that shit. You know, down through the chain of command—to me. Face to face, tell them. Most of the times I knew that these guys would never come back . . . most of them, at least. I had to look the brothers in the face and send them out on patrols. That's hard, Clay, sending a cat to the end of his future. And knowing it. When they would post the list of men killed in battle, I'd always look and see which brothers got killed. And I'd get to thinking about them . . . wondering . . . wondering . . . did they know there was no future? Did they know there was no future? Did they know that they had scraped and hustled trying to survive . . . only . . . only to be sent to some fuckin' unknown country to be killed in the prime of their lives?

[*Both* ROBERT *and* CLAY *are caught up in conversation, looking each other in the eyes.*]

So *now* the marines are sending me back to the Nam, to the motherfuckin' war, and I'm gonna have to tell more brothers to go out on patrols and see more brothers reach their *end*-dividual futures a million miles from home. [*reflects dreamily*] Raised all your life knowin' what place you were in . . . the last place . . . hustling and straining to survive all your goddam life, and then at the prime of your life sent to fight the motherfuckers' battles who has kicked you in the ass all your life.

[ROBERT *is really caught up in his monologue now. So is* CLAY, *whose eyes are flashing between* ROBERT, *the future and the past, daydreaming, nightdreaming, dreaming, roaming, remembering, remembering.*]

Congress goes through all kinds of weird changes to pass a civil-rights bill that shouldn't even be needed in a free country but would not hesitate, [*laughs*] not hes-i-tate, in passing laws to keep your ass in jail for eternity for refusing to fight their battles.

[*Now both* ROBERT *and* CLAY *sit straight up in their seats, both staring off into space, caught up in mutual thoughts and maybe even the flicker of the subways' lights outside the train.* ROBERT *turns toward* CLAY.]

Like I was saying 'bout Mr. Goodheart and all. Well, after I got out of Widener I went to Stoddart-Fleisher Junior High.

[ROBERT *laughs sarcastically while* CLAY *acknowledges the school, negatively.*]

You know what went on there. One big battle. Gang wars. Gang wars and more gang wars. I was supposed to go to Franklin High, man,

[*same look by both characters as on mentioning junior high school*]

but I knew if I went there I might not live to see twenty, so I took this test for Dobbins Vocational High and passed it, Clay. Got over the test and went there. I took up printing, man. Yeah . . . me . . . a motherfuckin' printer. [*change of mood*] Times were always hard, man, being poor and all. I'm not even going into that part . . . I know you know what I mean.

CLAY
[*shaking head*] Yeah, brother—dig it.

ROBERT
'Member when I used to come on your street . . . Flora Street, my brother and uncle selling fruits, man, shit [*laughing*] we had stolen that whole truckload of stuff. Money was a hustle, Clay. That's the whole thing, man. Money, you know!

34

[CLAY *is acting in agreement.* ROBERT *eyes the* HOMOSEXUAL *and points down the other end of the car.*]

See that punk sitting at the other end of the subway?

[CLAY *looks, follows his arm, nods head in agreement, with a mumbled "yeah."*]

[*defiantly*] What you say?

CLAY

[*uneasily*] Yeah, Robert. I see that cat. Stop pointing at him. I see him, all right.

ROBERT

Well, if that punk was to come down here and offer you twenty-five dollars to suck his dick . . . would you do it?

CLAY

Hell, no! I wouldn't take twenty-five dollars!

ROBERT

Aw, come on, man . . . really, now. How about fifty dollars or a hundred dollars?

CLAY

[*kind of shocked, but cool*] No, man, not for any amount of money. I just don't go that way.

ROBERT

Well, I don't go that way either. [*wild look on his face*] I don't hardly go that way, but if he offered me twenty-five dollars of U.S.A. currency, M–O–N–E–Y, I'd do it, Clay. I'd do it 'cause I know how hard money is to come by. That's what being poor means, man. That slender thread! That motherfuckin' slender thread. It would just be another hustle to me, Clay, . . . another hustle . . . another break in the threads, man.

[*They look at each other and break out laughing spontaneously.*]

You think I'm joking, don't you, Clay? [*changing mood*] Huh, huh, you think I'm not serious, don't you? Don't you? Don't you?

CLAY

I didn't say you weren't serious, Robert, it's just that . . .

ROBERT

[*breaking in*] Offer me twenty-five dollars, man. Shit, bet me twenty-five fuckin' dollars, Clay.

CLAY

Naw, brother. Come on . . . be cool. I know you can't be . . .

ROBERT

Twenty-five dollars, jack, twenty-five dollars so you'll understand, twenty-five dollars to show you how it is to be a poor black man. See, I'm a writer/poet, too.

CLAY

[*laughing kind of jokingly*] All right—O.K.

[ROBERT *runs across to where the* HOMOSEXUAL *has been sitting, biding his time. He stands the startled man up on his feet.* ROBERT *forcibly pulls down* HOMOSEXUAL's *zipper, hunts for his genitals.* CLAY, *astonished, runs over and struggles, finally pulls* ROBERT *away.* ROBERT *is now beginning to cry because he has failed to pull out the* HOMOSEXUAL's *genitals. The* HOMOSEXUAL *makes an attempt to get* ROBERT *back but is forcibly pushed away by* CLAY *onto the floor.* ROBERT, *with* CLAY *leading, returns to his seat.* HOMOSEXUAL *still on the floor. Train seems to come to a screeching halt.* HOMOSEXUAL *rises up from floor, wipes off his pants, goes back to seat, picks up suitcases and leaves through train door, ignoring* ROBERT *and* CLAY, *who remain seated,* ROBERT *with his head in hands.*]

[*raising his head*] Excuse me, Clay. I just wanted to show you that I was serious. Not joking but dead serious. 'Cause that's how bad the whole shit is. . . . And I knew you was a writer. . . . I thought that maybe you could write somethin' that would wake up a few more of the brothers to what's goin' down, 'cause I got to go back to the Nam, man. Ain't that a bitch? Back over there to the war. You [*pleadingly*] got to write stuff for the brothers, man. For the cats you knew at H. J. Widener. Don't be like your cousin, Clay. Don't be like that forgettin'-ass motherfucker.

CLAY

Don't worry, Robert, 'cause I'm not gonna let you or anybody down. Shit, tonight I wrote this [*pulls out papers which he has on him*] little piece at the party I went to. You know, everybody was shouting and dancing . . . having a good time and all, but I was caught up thinking about the old neighborhood and old times. Whatever happen to the old cats . . . Hell . . . you got anything to do? . . . Let's stay on this subway all goddamn night.

[*They both laugh.*]

I want you to hear this, Robert. I want you to hear it right now. Right in this subway car. I might even write some more stuff [*laughs*].

ROBERT

Shit, I might even help you, brother. . . . Go on and chirp.

[*Lights are flickering—motion of subway.*]

CLAY

[*rising from the seat, begins*] Homecookin'.

37

[CLAY *laughs along with* ROBERT, *then recites to audience.*
ROBERT *speaks interchangeably with* CLAY.]

I remember when nothing didn't really matter. When playgrounds were called squares with older cats playing A.S.S. or P.I.G. for two cents a game. And cried when they lost.

ROBERT

And cried when they lost two games in a row 'cause they had practiced fancy shots all week.

CLAY

Some of them could dunk, they were so mean. And Wilt was in eleventh grade out at Overbrook High. Guy Rodgers dribbled for North East while my junior-high coach cut me from the varsity team.

ROBERT

Randy Brown broke my fuckin' eyeglasses. My nose bled for two days stopping one morning to read about Birmingham explosions.

CLAY

Four girls, little girls dead. Little dead. Little dead girls, dead to be remembered. I remember when *Time* Magazine called my neighborhood The Jungle. Bill Cosby was one of its animals.

ROBERT

Gangs fought.

CLAY

Dick Clark kept us off his show and called it "American Bandstand," while we invented the twist two years ahead of time. I remember when *time* was getting there by 8:30 in the morning until 3:30 in the afternoon.

ROBERT

Leaving couldn't be too soon.

Tonto's partner was a masked man; his horse had a pink nose. Pink and silver with this cat in blue tights riding proudly. Queers wore women dresses.

ROBERT

My grandfather pointed out to me a whore who kissed me on the cheek. She had sores all down her legs and on her mouth. Running sores. Wet, running sores that smeared wetly on my face. And I grabbed her and kissed her back; my mother had been gone so long.

CLAY

Daddy died when I was six. I laughed at the funeral, wondering all the while what my little brother was thinking. Mom cried away from us up front. Alone. We in the back with Aunt Estelle. She got married again, and we called the cat Douglas. I learned about racism in the Boy Scouts. I remember turning teenager looking at TV Saturday night.

ROBERT

My father punching me in the mouth. My younger brother going to reform school.

CLAY

Nobody laughed anymore. Joyce Kennedy called me an "only child." I passed my college boards and picked up my draft card. College was in Washington D.C. I remember remembering life before the grownup twenty-one. Birds sang then, it seemed to me, if not The Jungle. My best friends laughed.

ROBERT

Sometimes.

CLAY

Atom bombs made no never mind.

ROBERT

Wines was purply bitter.

Reefer nonexistent. Speed a five letter word with a number underneath. Newark just before New York, void of flames and LeRoi Jones. Eyes to be laughed at.

ROBERT

Police to be eyed.

CLAY

Music men coughing up phlegm to masturbate on their horns. They were so weird. They were so good. Even the Lord seemed real. Even the real seemed possible and totally nonexistent. All at once, too. All at twice once upon a year. Once upon a star wished to at night for tomorrow to be like yesterday, not depending on today.

ROBERT

They were so good. Yet so bad I remember bad time. Bad Jungle.

CLAY

Bad times shimmering like the notes of a rainbow hummin'.

ROBERT

'Cause there wasn't no bags of gold hangin' anywhere. Just nickel bags of scag and reefer sold on the corner to too-young boys who got low to feel so high.

CLAY

Like the world who had forgotten their soulful presence. Some of them were dropouts never present: presently absent from school of school. Next school of life, then school of choice and opportunity to ever learn again.

ROBERT

Man, I never was one to do homework, anyway. Anyway.

CLAY

Anyway you turn you see a year. Pick it. Any year. Pick it.

They're all the same if you pray. Colors just change, and they don't really if you see properly. If you see Statues of Liberties on ten-cents postcards and still feel the same. Hoping she won't keep you after school or give you all F's. Big dead girl, dead to be remembered or forgotten just as quickly unless you're some western-world immigrant who was/is taught how to spell C–H–A–N–C–E. Chance to make it or get kicked up your ass. I remember having a chance to have no chance. Never getting off of a boat. Pushed off with a foot up my ass. Crying, grinning. Inside grinning. Outside frowning. . . . Learning how to dribble a basketball—good. Coach cutting me from the junior-high squad.

ROBERT

Pop getting laid off from work. Grandfather dying.

CLAY

Statue of Liberty lying with a smile on her face, hoping. Hoping she could come to life.

ROBERT

Rock to life hoping. Impossible to possible hoping.

CLAY

Hoping.

ROBERT

Hoping.

ROBERT and CLAY

Hoping.

CLAY

I remember hoping for prayer to have some meaning. Reverend Dunstin's wife divorced him for nonsupport. Earthquakes tremored San Francisco mornings. Angels peed in their sleep. And rained out never-never land.

41

ROBERT

Could I? Could I? . . .

CLAY

Think about tomorrow. Or dream about today remembering negative-sum-total yesterday. Who was I yesterday?

ROBERT

Who was I remembering?

CLAY

Remembering who wasn't I or them or we as a people wasn't songs. Songs that had no music sound. Sound that had no high or low. Songs that had no meaning or sight. Sad songs can't be wrongs.

ROBERT

Lord's Prayer songs.

CLAY

Psalms.

ROBERT

Twenty-third Psalm.

CLAY

Psalm songs. Revelations should be songs. Revelations can't be wrongs. Or right if they're blind, deaf, and dumb.

ROBERT

Silent songs.

CLAY

Silent songs sung on silent nights by shepherds tending their flock, praying for a white Christmas—and they had never heard of snow . . . or freedom. If I remember.

ROBERT

She had been gone away for so—

42

CLAY

long. And my stomach was starting to make that particular growl sound. That Tarzan-movie cannibal sound.

ROBERT

White people running to get out of the neighborhood quickly. Store windows being smashed. Choice U.S.-Inspected anything temporarily free. Can I get a witness?

CLAY

Clicking camera sounds recording picture files for future soul kids to see themselves in color if their eyesight had been in black and white. I remember black and white. Willie Mays hitting number five hundred. Mickey Mantle retiring. Straws that had elastic bands.

ROBERT

Waiting in line to shit.

CLAY

Ex-Lax in my pocket.

ROBERT

Cork in my hand.

CLAY

Elephants copulating to bring about a new ton. Rainy days in April with no clothes on. Cutting class and wrist.

ROBERT

Dying.

CLAY

Reliving. Finding out I was never born.

ROBERT

Celebrating birthdays.

CLAY

Surprise parties. White turtleneck sweaters with hidden tape recorders. Milk in a plastic glass. Dinosaurs saying "We Shall Overcome."

ROBERT

Stepin Fetchit busting his nuts.

CLAY

Shirley Temple ugly and to the right. White kids hairy and to the left. Laughing at dinosaurs. Feeding them berries.

ROBERT

Jesus Christ wishing he could African twist.

CLAY

Virgin Mary discovering B.C. pills, camels farting and blasting off one hump. The sky falling. My wife vomiting up her breakfast. Last night being so long to get to this morning. I remember this morning when the daylight first showed its ass. Making last night an oncoming past. All creation a blurred looking glass. Looking backward at nothing but the present second.

ROBERT

If you could afford a decent watch. Or a decent apartment. Or a decent bed to fall asleep and dream on. If I could fall asleep. But I'm not . . . asleep now.

CLAY

I remember now. School teacher spelling

ROBERT

N–O–W.

CLAY

Bushy-head black cat's putting "Freedom" before it. Chambers Brother's singing that it was the time.

ROBERT

Time calling my neighborhood The Jungle.

44

CLAY

Martin Luther King shouting "It really doesn't matter with me now." Me agreeing with him. Bullets speeding toward a kind man's neck. Blood spattered upon a motel door.

ROBERT

Race wars. Race wars. Young bloods killed in Vietnam. Little kids running from nasty napalm. Lights flickering on and off. Clubs on my heads. The radio slightly off station.

CLAY

This disc jockey hollering "Good Morning. Get up, World. Time for Work. This is WNOW." My God, the day is coming, I can see it in my mirror. Next year I'll be a one year older.

ROBERT

A one year older.

CLAY

I got this strange feeling in my balls.

ROBERT

They're boiling.

CLAY

Having ESP. with my original womb. Africa flashes by. I knew I could beat drums.

ROBERT

I'm a good farmer, too.

CLAY

Singing while I work. Singing while we work. What is time? What is a second? What is an eight-hour day? Songhay my Nation 'tis of Thee. Oh, how I worship the *sun*. A long-gone villager returns to the village. He says . . .

ROBERT

What's happening is across the sea.

CLAY

That he's been there.

ROBERT

Attack! Attack!

CLAY

Attack! Chains around my ankle and my neck. White-skinned people. I . . . I remember white-skin people fondling my dick and balls out in public.

ROBERT

Am I being sold?

CLAY

I remember being sold. Being worked and whipped. Whipped but not beaten. Stars over Jerusalem. Easter Sunday Resurrection.

ROBERT

Resurrection City.

CLAY

Being shot off after a funky broadway jam. Waking up one morning to know who I was or am. Past Perfect Present Future Am.

ROBERT

Philly, North Philly, Harlem, Watts Am.

CLAY

Remembering am. Today I woke up remembering when nothing didn't really matter.

ROBERT

She had been gone away so so long. . . . [*pause . . . drifts off, saying*] Ain't no future, man. Ain't no future, man. . . . Ain't no future man . . .

46

CLAY

[*after watching* ROBERT *drift off, continues reading poem*] And all she left was a song. Sad songs. Sorry songs. Sad Sorry can't be wrongs. Psalm songs. Twenty-third psalm. Shadow-of-death songs, where I belonged. Fried chicken taste so goddam good. Watermelon ain't bad. Porks not good for our health. You know what chitlins are, hogs fart too. Gentle aromas easing out of the kitchen. My wife cooks good. . . . Homecookin' . . . 'cause last night I really did my homework. I really did my homework. I really did my. I really did. I really. I . . .

Lights dim out
End

ANDREW
A Play in Remembrance

CHARACTERS 🎭

PAUL

BILLY

ANDREW

The characters are three black dudes between eighteen and twenty living in the North Philly slums. These brothers act very hip. They are bad motherfuckers, not to be messed with at all. They are not to be dressed sloppily or dirty but casually, clean—as in very clean dude.

SETTING 🎭

North Philadelphia at night. A street sign (bigger than life) represents the corner of Twenty-ninth and Ridge Avenue. PAUL *is on stage.*

PAUL

This ain't no play, man. I'm tryin' to find my main man, Andrew. The cat was here about a second or so ago. Hey Andrew? Where you at, man? No shit, man, where you at? Come on out, jack. I ain't gon' move on you again. Where you at, man?

BILLY

[*entering*] What's happenin', dude!

PAUL

You seen Andrew, man?

51

BILLY

Naw, man, but I got some dynamite grass and . . .

PAUL

. . . This ain't no play, man. . . . You seen Andrew or what?

BILLY

Yeah, I . . . I seen the dude, man . . . but not today. I mean, I seen the cat a second or so ago.

PAUL

You've seen the cat, man?

BILLY

Naw, not really, man, but *Yeah* if you can dig me . . . I mean, maybe if we could sit down somewhere and rap or . . .

PAUL

Look man, I said this ain't no joke.

BILLY

I ain't joking man, I got some grass and banana paper now . . .

PAUL

Now is *over*, man. You know that. Things ain't never gonna be like they was.

BILLY

All we gotta do is talk, man. Just talk, that's all. I ain't askin' no favors, Paul.

PAUL

I ain't asking no favors either, Billy. I'm askin' you have you seen my man, Andrew?

BILLY

I said about a second or so ago, remember?

PAUL

Remember *what*, man?

BILLY

Remember when we was kids and belonged to Troop 465 down in the church basement? 'Member that time when me and you and . . . and . . . and . . .

PAUL

Andrew!

BILLY

Yeah. . . . yeah, Andrew. Remember when we all got left behind on that camping trip? We was too young to dig on what was comin' down then.

PAUL

I . . . I don't understand what's comin' down now, man. The cat was here just a second ago. Right here. Standin' right here in front of me, rapping.

BILLY

Yeah, the cat *could* rap his ass off. I really hated havin' to mess with the dude . . .

PAUL

What? What you say, man?

BILLY

You heard me, Paul, man. You remember what we had to put down on the cat. He wasn't from the neighborhood anymore, you know. He wasn't part of the group, man. Plus he was in the Zulu Nation.

PAUL

The Zulu N— . . . man, we never got *questioned* even for what came down on the dude. Before he moved he used to live right next door to me.

BILLY

I spotted Andy walkin' down the street. He was all right wit me, but you remember how it was I . . . I said, "What's your name, brotherman . . ."

PAUL

We was all laughing, too.

BILLY

Even Andy. I said, "where you from, brotherman?"

PAUL

He was comin' to see my sister.

BILLY

I . . . I said, "Where you goin', brotherman?" And he said, . . .

ANDREW

[*entering*] Yawl know who I am. Andy! I just moved from around here a second ago. What's happenin'?

BILLY

You, brotherman, hear you gon Zulu Nation.

ANDREW

Yeah, I gotta live man, you know.

PAUL

You know something else, man?

ANDREW

What's that, Paul?

PAUL

It ain't that easy to jam my sister, man.

ANDREW

What you talkin' 'bout, Paul, man? This is *me*, Andy, man. I use to live next door, jack. Your sister's my woman.

BILLY

Where you from, brotherman?

54

ANDREW

I'm from here, yawl know that.

PAUL

I don't know *nothin'*, man.

BILLY

Where you from brotherman?

ANDREW

Nowhere then.

BILLY

What?

ANDREW

I said nowhere then.

PAUL

Uh huh, well *nowhere then* is getting stronger, man.

ANDREW

Look here, yawl, I ain't got no time to . . .

BILLY

You right, man, you ain't got no time. No time unless you do some mean rapping.

ANDREW

About what?

PAUL

About *when.*

ANDREW

When what?

BILLY

When you was *really* living.

ANDREW

I was born next door to Paul down here in the projects. And I knew when my family moved from here that I was never gonna be able to come back.

PAUL

But you're here, Andy, man. You right back here with us.

BILLY

You remember us, man. Or do you just remembering jamming Paul's sister, huh? You 'member us?

ANDREW

Yeah, Billy, you know I remember yawl. I used to be one of yawl.

BILLY

You used to be living, jack.

ANDREW

And when I was, I used to love you cats.

PAUL

And when you was, you belonged to the Zulu Nation.

ANDREW

And when I was, I used to party strong with you cats.

BILLY

And when you was, you moved to another neighborhood.

ANDREW

And when I was, I used to gang war hard with you cats.

PAUL

And when you was, you made the mistake of coming on back.

ANDREW

And when I was, I used to drink wine on the corner with you cats.

BILLY

And when you was, you use to hate the Zulu Nation.

56

ANDREW

And when I was, I use to love all you cats in the projects.

PAUL

And when you was, we had to kill you.

BILLY

It was like a thing, you know. A thing that had to be done, you know. Like even now I remember how you looked and how you fought, but damn I mean . . .

ANDREW

Like it was kinda funny before yawl killed me, cause we had been steady rapping. And after I died . . . shit, way after I died, I wasn't even mad at yawl.

PAUL

We was all laughing, too.

ANDREW

I knew yawl was gonna ice me, man. I couldn't believe it, you understand. But I knew.

BILLY

I knew too, man. And we did too. Shot the shit out him. Knocked him back 'bout two sidewalk squares.

PAUL

Even Andy was laughing.

ANDREW

'Cause the shit was funny. It was really some funny shit. You kept asking me them questions. I knew I couldn't win.

PAUL

Naw, man, you could have won. You could have won big, too, man. Real big.

BILLY

We had the wine ready to celebrate, man, ice cold Ripple wine. We was all hoping you'd come through.

ANDREW

Naw, I couldn't have won. Them questions was getting to me, I . . .

PAUL

The thing wasn't *even* to *win*, man. It . . . it was to remember, see. That's where you blew your cool, man. In remembering.

ANDREW

In remembering. Now wait a minute. I remembered. I did remember, man. Everything you asked me I had an answer.

BILLY

Yeah, you had the right answers, too.

PAUL

'Cept they was so right they was wrong.

ANDREW

Wait a minute, now. So right they was wrong. Where yawl comin' from, my whole rap was very right. Might of fact, it was mean.

PAUL and **BILLY**

Naw, man! Naw, man! Naw, man! Naw, man!

ANDREW

It was right, man. I know it was. Yawl had just made up your minds to off me anyway. You know I could dig it. I died anyway!

PAUL and **BILLY**

Naw man! You wrong, Andy. Naw man!

ANDREW

Wrong. I was right. Ask me them questions again. Shit, I ain't got nothin' to lose.

PAUL

You ain't got nothing to gain either, man.

ANDREW

I don't know about that. Go 'head and ask me them questions again.

BILLY

Where you from brotherman?

ANDREW

Richard Allen Projects, across the bridge from Strawberry Mansion.

BILLY

Where you from brotherman?

ANDREW

From right down here wit yawl. Next door to my main man, Paul.

BILLY

Where you from brotherman?

ANDREW

From . . . from . . . I was born in Charleston, South Carolina, in 1949 and my great-great grandpop was a slave who spoke fluent *Ibo*.

PAUL

So! So!

BILLY

Ibo? Man, where you comin' from, brotherman?

ANDREW

From another neighborhood. Another bag. Another time, man, when niggers was talking Yoruba up in the hills.

PAUL

Cool it, Andy man. This ain't no play, jack.

ANDREW

I know, man, but dig on this performance. Like . . . like I was from another neighborhood and I had to play the part 'cause . . .

BILLY

'Cause we weren't playing, Andy. Where were you goin'
brotherman?

ANDREW

I . . . I was goin' to die and I knew it, so I forgot about Paul's
younger sister and how much she dug me. I forgot about all you
niggers and the boss times we had had together. I started remembering.

BILLY

Remembering what, man? You still got shot.

ANDREW

Remembering how you cats danced and sang, and how you cats
walked down the street and stood on the block and messed with
the women, and . . .

PAUL

Like you was messing with my sister, huh?

ANDREW

Naw Paul, you know your sister had my nose wide open.

BILLY

Look man, the shit is too long already. By now you was long
dead.

ANDREW

Maybe so, Billy, but I had remembered everything we had done.

PAUL

Dance like we use to dance, brotherman.

[ANDREW *does the Philly Dog, African Twist, and Popcorn;*
PAUL *and* BILLY *join in.*]

Sing like we use to sing, brotherman.

[ANDREW *sings* "There was a Time" *by James Brown;* PAUL *and* BILLY *join in laughing, screaming the imitation of the instruments with their voices.*]

Walk down the street like we use to walk, brotherman.

[ANDREW *soul struts.*]

BILLY

Mess with the women, brotherman.

ANDREW

Hey momma, you sure do look good . . . to me. Umm nmm you really P–H–A–T—phat for days.

[*They all laugh.*]

BILLY

[*still laughing*] And . . . some nights alone I used to get to crying, thinking about what went down. 'Cause . . . 'cause you was really hip, and me and Paul never got busted or even questioned about the killing.

PAUL

[*still laughing*] And my sister, man, she came up to my room one night and ask me did I know who killed you. And I thought about the shit and didn't really know . . . didn't even know why it happened at all except it had to happen. I told her that I'd find out through the grapevine for her but I *never* did. .

ANDREW

I never did either understand what I didn't remember. It seemed to me that I remembered everything like it was. I mean, I ain't making no excuse 'cause the language I was talking was stone Ibo and yawl was rapping some mean Yoruba. And . . .

PAUL

And all that night my sister was asking everybody, "Have you seen Andrew? He said he'd be over in about an hour from when he called."

ANDREW

I even remember tellin' her that. And getting on the bus to make it on over there chained and silent.

BILLY

I spotted you gettin' off the bus and I told Paul to check you out. We was just joking at first, but when you . . .

ANDREW

I looked in both your eyes and dug on what was coming down. And somewhere I dug we was once brothers. Friends.

BILLY

We was just joking at first, but when you started talking that . . . that . . .

ANDREW

Yeah, that . . . that what?

PAUL

When you started rapping that goddam stupid ass Yoruba that the niggers talk up your neighborhood, I mean we had to off you, man, 'cause . . .

BILLY

'Cause really we could understand what you was saying, but we didn't know where you was comin' from . . . or maybe we knew where you *was coming from* and *was goin'*.

ANDREW

And I belonged to the Zulu Nation on the other side of time, and I was going to see Paul's sister, and my name was Andrew.

PAUL

And your name *had been Andrew* but your talking said you

didn't remember your friends, man, 'cause my name was still Billy and Paul's name was still Paul and this neighborhood was still this neighborhood, and all you had [*hits* BILLY's *hands*] to do was *hit our hands* and keep on getting up like you would have done before.

BILLY

But naw, man, you had to mess with us and—

ANDREW

Mess with yawl, man, I came over to see Paul's sister. How was I messing wit yawl?

BILLY

'Cause if you had really remembered who we was, really remembered *what we was* and where *you* was, and how you had been part of that [*they hit hands again*] you would of just hit our hands and went on over to Paul's house.

PAUL

You was out of your territory, man. By messing with us. Talking to us you *was* really out of your territory, man! You was from the Zulu Nation, man, not the Richard Allen Projects anymore, you understand?

BILLY

We had to off you for trespassing against us, Andy, man.

ANDREW

And after I died, man, I . . . I learned to love yawl, too. I looked on either side of the city and really felt that we was really something once, before the long trip over. Like it was funny as shit while we was talking. And after I died I was never really mad. Not . . . not . . . once I just didn't understand us crowded close together in that project not knowing what each other was saying, like sorry Africans on a slave ship chained and silent during the long trip over. . . . *Fluent* Ibo.

63

PAUL and BILLY

So!

ANDREW

Fluent Yoruba!

PAUL and BILLY

So!

ANDREW

And I died! [*walks off stage puzzled*]

PAUL

You've *seen* Andrew?

BILLY

Yeah, not really, I mean if you can dig on me.

PAUL

You've *seen* the dude, man?

BILLY

Maybe if we could go somewhere and sit down, like I got some mean reefer and some banana paper, you can roll if you want to, now.

PAUL

Now is *over*, man. You know that. Things ain't never gonna be like they was 'cause . . . 'cause [*turns to audience*] this ain't no play, man.

Lights dim out
End

Of Being Hit

CHARACTERS ✂

HOLLY, *well-built brown-skinned man around forty, janitor*
DUNCAN, *average-built man same age, janitor*
MR. WILSON, *early fifties*

SETTING ✂

This play employs simultaneous staging. The main set,
which takes up most of the stage, is in the design of an
office room filled with a desk and file cabinets. Yet in front
of this set, out toward the audience, as if it were aproned
off, is the dramatic image of boxing ring ropes which give
the audience the illusion of looking through these ring
ropes in order to view the play. There should be two sets of
pails and mops on the main set for the two janitors to use
during the action that takes place.

HOLLY
[*shadow boxing*] You do the best you can, man. Sometimes you
get the breaks and sometimes you don't. Then you just die of a
kidney ailment one day, that's all.

DUNCAN
[*mopping floor*] Where at you gonna die, Holly. Huh? Where
at? and when?

HOLLY
What from? Simple, man. Them punches to the midsection.
They got a way of comin' back on you weeks later sometimes.

67

Years later, too. Uh huh, years later—I should know. [*clutches midsection*] Whew!

DUNCAN

Where at Holly? I asked you where at. Where at?

HOLLY

Oh, at uh Providence Hospital in a ward section. Providence Hospital. Smallpox ward . . .

DUNCAN

Smallpox ward! Whaat?

HOLLY

Yeah, smallpox, man. That's what they used to say was the matter. Goldie Blumberg, the promoter, said other fighters turned me down like I had smallpox, or somethin'. I was what you call a spoiler. A spoiler. Ever heard of Willie Troy?

DUNCAN

Willie Troy? Willie? Yeah, uh middleweight, right. Back in the fifties, I think. He was pretty good, too. You fought him too, huh?

HOLLY

What you mean *too*, man. I don't have no reason to . . .

DUNCAN

O.K. All right, I was, I was just joking with ya, Holly. Fought Willie Troy, huh?

HOLLY

Damn right, man. But that wasn't the hurter, man. Now the thing that hurt me most was that—

DUNCAN

Wait a minute, Holly. Slow down a second. You said you fought Willie Troy back in the fifties. How . . . how did you uh make out?

HOLLY

Made out O.K. Pretty good. O.K.

DUNCAN

Come on, Holly. I mean, how did you uh do? Did you win the fight or lose?

HOLLY

I won ninety-five fights, man. Naw, I fought ninety-five fights, you see. Won sixty-four with six draws. Man, I hated draws . . .

DUNCAN

Look, man, I asked you how did you make out? Did you win or lose? What's the matter, did you get knocked out or something?

HOLLY

[*loud, mad*] Knocked out! I was never knocked out, never! You hear that, jack, never. Uh—knocked off my feet once though, but never—

DUNCAN

Win or lose? Holly. Win or lose? Win or lose?

HOLLY

Lose? Uh [*counts fingers*] thirty-one fights, I reckon.

DUNCAN

Troy. Willie Troy . . .

HOLLY

[*grinning*] Knocked ole Troy out, Duncan. Knocked the cat out. Old Goldie Blumberg, you know, the promoter, he . . . he said Willie Troy just ran on away from me then. Just was running away from a rematch. Grapevine had it out I couldn't punch. Didn't have no punch. That . . . that I was a soft touch.

DUNCAN

Guess Troy didn't think so. Bet he didn't, huh?

69

HOLLY

Yeah, he knew. They all knew soon enough. It was just that I wasn't no slugger.

DUNCAN

A boxer, huh? Like Sugar Ray.

HOLLY

Fought six champions.

DUNCAN

Six championship fights. Man, what you doin' sweeping floors with me then? Jesus Christ, six champion fights.

HOLLY

Naw, man, they wasn't no championship fights.

DUNCAN

Whaat? You said you fought six champions—Sugar Ray.

HOLLY

Sugar Ray! Fought him too, Sugar Ray.

DUNCAN

[*jerking his head as if he hears a sound*] Wait a minute, Holly. Stop that boxing around and hold on to that broom. Think I hear Mr. Wilson comin'. You know he don't like seeing nobody standin' around on the job.

[HOLLY *stops shadow boxing and grabs broom, starts making sweeping motions. They both pause, working until the scare has passed.*]

Now what was you talking about?

HOLLY

Uh . . . hu . . . uh . . . damn, I really can't remember what I was saying. Uh . . . yeah . . . well my son comes in my room and he ask me for some money. A couple of dollars. He's

70

twenty-one, you know. Takes after his maw, kinda fat. Not too much, though. Now his sister . . .

DUNCAN
Naw you wasn't talking 'bout that. You was saying something 'bout fighting.

HOLLY
Yeah, I used to be a fighter. A middleweight. Professional, too. After I won the Golden Gloves in forty-seven, turned pro a year later.

DUNCAN
You said you fought Sugar Ray??

HOLLY
You see, Duncan, fight game's a funny business. Like they expects you to go out there and get hurt. All cut up—

DUNCAN
Sugar Ray? Sugar Ray, Holly! Sugar Ray.

HOLLY
Like I was what they called a . . . a . . . counterpuncher. Not a slugger or a boxer but a counterpuncher. [*puts broom back down on desk*] I didn't call them. They had to call me. And when they did, I had a punch waiting for 'em. A punch right from behind the *counter*. Know what I mean, huh?

DUNCAN
[*exasperated*] What do you mean, Holly?

HOLLY
Try and hit me, Duncan? Put down your broom and try and hit me. Come on, Duncan. Come on, try and hit me.

DUNCAN
Holly, you must be joking. Old man Wilson hear us up here scuffling about, he'll fire us in a second.

71

[*dancing around*] Come on, Dunc. Try and hit me. I wanna show you what I mean about a counterpuncher.

DUNCAN

Man, I follow fighting. Don't you think I know what a counterpunch is.

HOLLY

Yeah, I know you knows, Duncan. But you ain't never been in the ring with a counterpuncher. Especially not one like me, have you?

DUNCAN

[*laughing and putting down his mop*] Christ, I must be looney as a bat boxing you here at the job. Well, if we gonna box tonight we might as well do it up right. [*imitating an announcer*] In this corner [*points at* HOLLY, *who is jumping in place with serious expression on face*] . . . in this corner, with red trunks and white shoes, weighing one hundred sixty pounds even, Holly.

[HOLLY *raises both hands as if to a crowd.*]

In the opposite corner, of course, wearing green satin trunks with black patent leather shoes with felt tips, weighing in at one sixty even, the great Duncan. [*raises hands imitating* HOLLY]

HOLLY

Try and hit me, Duncan. Come on, try and hit me.

DUNCAN

I can't, man. You know that.

HOLLY

Try and hit me, man. Come on now. I'm ready for you now. Come on, Dunc.

DUNCAN

What kind of fighter were you, man? You know I can't hit you yet.

HOLLY

Can't hit me yet? Why not, man? How come? You scared to or something? I scare ya?

DUNCAN

Naw, you don't scare me. It's just that the bell ain't rung yet, that's all.

HOLLY

The bell? What bell you talking 'bout, man? Ain't no bell in here.

DUNCAN

Now look, I said I'd box you. But only if you ring the bell, Holly. I mean I got pride, you know I'm a proud boxer, jack, you understand!

HOLLY

[laughing] All right, all right, I'll ring the bell. Ding! Ding! Now come on out and get whipped.

[DUNCAN circles HOLLY, waiting for an opening to punch through. Suddenly he throws a big right hand, which HOLLY expertly blocks. HOLLY throws about six punches at DUNCAN in a loud flash. Each punch is accompanied with POW POW BOOO BOOM POW OPOW.]

Try again, Dunc. Try again.

[DUNCAN throws another punch—same thing happens.]

Try again, baby. Try me one mo gin.

[Same thing takes place.]

73

DUNCAN

[*amazed at* HOLLY's *speed*] Wheeew, man, you . . . you still fast as lighting. How old you, man? We must be about the same age, huh?

HOLLY

I don't know how old you are, but I'm forty.

DUNCAN

Forty? You two years older'n me. Don't seem like it, though. Damn.

HOLLY

No big thing . . . forty. It's how you feel inside that counts. Try and hit me again, O.K.?

DUNCAN

O.K. One more time and that's it. [*Throws punch at* HOLLY.]

HOLLY

[*throws flurries of six punches each, saying the names*] Paddy Young, Spider Webb, Mile Sabage, Johnny Bratter, Ernie Durrando, Ray Robinson, RAY ROBINSON. RAY ROBINSON! [*furious punches*]

DUNCAN

[*stops him from punching out so hard and wild at the very atmosphere surrounding him*] Whoa now, Holly. Calm down, man. Be cool now. You gotta think about this job, now. I don't mind you messing around none or nothing but you gonna make us both lose our jobs. What you got against Ray Robinson, man? Wow. You was scaring me there for a while, punching out like that. Huh, Holly? Holly, what ya got against Sugar Ray? You said ya fought him once.

HOLLY

Yeah, that's right, once. I uh lost a close decision to him in fifty-one. Real close. Real close.

DUNCAN

Blew your mind huh, losing to Sugar . . .

HOLLY

Losing. Man, I won . . . I only lost . . . losing! The cat,
Sugar Ray was about the meanest coolest cat there was, Dunc.
Wasn't no excuse losing to him. People still dug me and all.
'Cept that . . . that!

DUNCAN

Yeah . . . yeah?

HOLLY

'Cept that . . . you see, Duncan, the fight game's a funny
business.

DUNCAN

You said that before now.

HOLLY

Well it is a funny business. It was down in Miami. The fight
was. Me and Sugar Ray Robinson. The great Sugar Ray Robinson against me. I . . . I was kinda nervous before the fight but
not that much. I knew myself, see . . .

DUNCAN

Knew yourself? What has that got to do with it?

HOLLY

You just can't go into a ring with somebody like Ray Robinson
without knowing who you are, understand? 'Cause you know
who he is, dig it. And you know what he can do to ya. Real
quick, too. He don't waste no time playing around. Ca Pow,
that's the show.

DUNCAN

Yeah, yeah, go on, go on. The fight, the fight!

HOLLY

Well . . . I was in good shape. Reflexes sharp as a tacknail.

Surprised myself that night. Fought real good. Real good. Lost a close decision. Real close decision.

DUNCAN

Yeah, well . . . you know . . . that's the way it goes, you know. Win a few, lose a few. You fought good anyway.

HOLLY

But that wasn't the hurter, man. That wasn't the hurter. After the announcer gave out the decision, Sugar came over to me and told me I gave 'em a hell of a fight. Hell of a battle. That's the way he was, all class. All class. New York, New York. You know.

DUNCAN

The hurter, man. What was the hurter?

HOLLY

The hurter? Yes. The hurter was that the word got out about my fight game.

DUNCAN

That grapevine you was talking earlier about . . .

HOLLY

The grapevine, yeah. That's what they called it, too, the grapevine. Word was out that I wasn't no soft touch but a dangerous fighter.

DUNCAN

That bad, huh . . .

HOLLY

It . . . it became so bad there were days I thought I'd never get another fight. That bad. [*unexpectedly takes off his shirt and undershirt*]

DUNCAN

Holly, are you drunk or somethin'? Now what you go take off your shirt for?

76

HOLLY

I was considered a spoiler.

DUNCAN

Put your damn shirt back on. The matter wit you! You funny or something?

HOLLY

You ain't laughing, are you? Anyway, what's wrong with taking my shirt off? Lest it bothers you.

DUNCAN

Lest it bothers me. Why you take your shirt off, Holly? If you keep acting crazy I might have to call Wilson up here myself. Wow!

HOLLY

The hurter, man. Like this was me. My body. All I had.

DUNCAN

Still don't mean you gotta undress in here in front of me. Startin' to wonder about you now.

HOLLY

Just 'cause I show you my chest I funny, huh? I showed this chest ninety-five times in the ring. Didn't nobody think nothing. Where was your chest then? Where was it? Was . . . was Sugar Ray gay, man, just 'cause he showed himself, huh? Was Sugar Ray gay?

DUNCAN

Was Sugar Ray gay! Holly you feeling all right, man? Was Sugar Ray gay!

HOLLY

He had beautiful legs, didn't he? Didn't he?

DUNCAN

Look here, Holly. I think we better get back to working. Was Sugar . . .

HOLLY

Well, they was. That's what my wife said after the fight. She said he had beautiful legs.

DUNCAN

That's your wife's problem, jack. Don't mean I got to say it. Or you. Now get to work.

HOLLY

All right, all right, I was just making fun, that's all. Just making a joke. That's all. Forget it, O.K.? Forget it.

DUNCAN

All right, I'll uh forget it. Come on now, let's finish up this job, solid.

HOLLY

Be with you in a second, Dunc; first I got to make it to the bathroom for a second. [*picks up shirt, undershirt*] My kidneys, you understand. Nineteen years in the ring.

[*When* HOLLY *leaves to go to the bathroom,* DUNCAN *is just standing up there sweeping the floor and he's whistling. Then he hears the noise and* MR. WILSON *comes in and* DUNCAN *tries to ignore him, acting like he's really doing work. He speeds up his sweeping.*]

MR. WILSON

How you doin', Duncan?

DUNCAN

How you doing? Pretty nice night, huh?

MR. WILSON

Hey, Duncan, how about that Holly, huh? Died on us, huh? Guess he just didn't want to come into work anymore.

78

DUNCAN

[*being cool*] Yeah, that was something—that was something.

MR. WILSON

[*taking newspaper from back pocket*] That's something about Holly, a number one contender. It says here in his obituary. [*unfolds it*] It says here in this here obituary that . . . that Holly fought in the ring for nineteen years. Nineteen years he fought without gettin' a crack at the big money. At the championship. Know what, Duncan, well I use to ask the man . . . I'd say, "Hey Holly, your luck just wasn't with you back in them prize fighting days." [*laughs*] All Holly'd do was shrug my question off and keep on gettin' on up. Know what I mean? That's the way he was. Never got a break but he just kept on gettin' on up. Kept on living, I guess. Says here he died from his kidneys.

DUNCAN

[*still sweeping*] Just like he said he would!

MR. WILSON

Providence Hospital. General Ward. I . . . I could tell he had lost some weight lately? Humph! Nineteen years of being hit. Nineteen years of gettin' smashed in the face without getting the one punch over. Duncan, you know he told me one night. He told me one night that he was in the encyclopedia. [*laughs*] The boxing encyclopedia. Brought it in to work to . . . to prove it to me. Wonder how much money he made in the ring off of ninety-five fights? Wonder where it went. Hell, I was payin' him $1.86 an hour. Less than you, Dunc. [*laughs*] Yeah, less than you. [*walks out of room*]

[DUNCAN *freezes facing audience.* HOLLY *has walked back onstage, fumbling with his zipper, finally closing it.*]

79

HOLLY

You know, Dunc. The fun part about boxing was the press pictures. The women loved 'em, know what I mean. The photographer would take three poses. First was one with your hands up on guard like this. [*pauses and strikes the pose he has just described until he is satisfied that he has it right*] The second one was a close-up of just the side of your face, like. [*presses and poses once again*] The third one, now that's the one I liked the best. [*lights dimming*] The third one was a close-up of the front of your face smiling. [*smiles broadly*] Just smiling. [*hands up in exultation to the sky.*]

Lights dim out
End

MARS
Monument to the
Last Black Eunuch

CHARACTERS ♪

BLACK MAN, *middle-aged laborer.*

CHORUS, *five to eight people who play other roles throughout the play. One of the female members must be able to sing extremely well—extremely well as in Aretha or Nina or even Nancy Wilson. The scat-singing part should be done very creatively and effectively. Nothing is worse than having a so-called good actress with a bad voice. Preferably, a singer should have the role. Also, the* CHORUS *should have body movements that are exaggerated; after all, this is a monumental play. And all the characters are monumental (bigger than life).*

WIFE, *called "baby" by* BLACK MAN. WIFE *has only one line, at the end of the play. Throughout the play she does movement with her body. Her body should reflect thought patterns.* WIFE *should be played by a strong actress, who can demand power and stage presence through her body.*

BAND

WOMAN'S VOICE

SETTING ♪

A playground with a very large (gigantic) sliding board with a large swing connected underneath the middle of the board between the ladder and the sliding part. WIFE *sits in the swing.* CHORUS *should have rhythm (as in rhythm and blues).*

COSTUMES ❦

CHORUS *females wear long robes which are bed sheets that have been tie-dyed (African tie-dyed).* CHORUS *males are dressed like the mud men of Australia, with gray-beige mud on their bare chests and legs. They wear shorts, and they look like false faces. Their heads are shaved.*

Prologue

CHORUS

[*sings African-style chant*]

Monument to
to to to
the last
  black
  eunuch
Monument, monument
    to the last
      the last
      the last
        black
        eunuch

Act I

BLACK MAN *is at apron of stage left shaping a piece of scrap material into a work of art. While he is constructing, a voice is singing in the background. When he finishes, he exits.* CHORUS *assembles onstage wearing white working uniforms and walking like robots, making mechanical movements. They put together the set, which turns out to be a*

children's playground. They disrobe and take various posi-
tions on the playground. (Lights come on.) CHORUS *be-*
comes children playing games. BLACK MAN *and* WIFE *enter.*
WIFE *goes and sits down on swing.* BLACK MAN *begins rap-*
ping.]

BLACK MAN

Maybe it's because we're married, baby. Maybe it's because
we've been married so long . . . you know . . . like the whole
routine and shit, that it's kinda become a standard . . . like
"Moon River" . . . with us. Between us. "Moon River" between us . . . "Moon River" between us. Noise between the
scratched-up grooves with Jerry Butler groanin' over and over
again 'Moon River" . . . "Moon River." 'Cause I almost ex-
pect to hear the disc jockey say: "One More Time." And I
really don't know if I can take it again! . . . Really, I guess it's
hard . . . kinda hard for you to understand . . . you bein' in
the church and all, but damn . . . I mean . . . a man has got
to see if he can *see* for real, once. Really see if he can *see* . . .
if he can feel, if he can stand on the Boardwalk naked, maybe
except for a make shift loincloth. Ha ha. Except for one jock
strap, and see . . . see and feel . . . if the moon can pull a
psyche on his body just like it psyches those stupid waves—day
in, day out . . . in . . . out . . . high tide . . . low tide . . .
ebb tide . . . Wednesday . . . Thursday . . . Tuesday . . .
Sunday. . . . For Christ's sakes, Sunday too, with that old
minstrel Uncle Ben peddlin' his stupid instant rice to Sapphire
over the supermarket behind the Kingfish's back. You know,
he died broke . . . the Kingfish. . . . The cat who played the
Kingfish died . . . died . . . died broke, busted, robbed, lynched
. . . the whole Western-world bit. But I laughed at him, baby,
me and Fred and Briggs and Jackie.

And a lot of people saw the cat, if just for once, and we laughed
at him. . . . Even Andy laughed at the cat, 'cause Kingfish was

always tryin' to *us* and move uptown to the high-rent district. I remember roaches standin' proudly right out in the middle of the living room floor. . . . And they was singing, baby. Singing the Lord's Prayer better than the Wings Over Jordan choir. I was so weak that I just stood there proud they had chosen my house. They didn't even notice me and then suddenly . . . real fast like . . . this thought came to my head and I said out loud . . . real loud . . . [*loudly*] I am the roach. He that can withstand DDT. The meat. The wieny. Faster than a flying bullet. More powerful than an enraged elephant. . . ROACH-MAN. And the roaches, they like to died, they was so happy they was scampering about so. While one by one got his ass crushed by the soles of my shoes, and I ain't sorry about a damn thing, baby. Shit. No! Not when I was God. Not when I was the roach. Maker of all life somewhere. If just somewhere and someplace. Somebody's home place. Homeland. Goddammit, where am I from? Who are my great-grand relatives? Who is related to me? Am I Am We? Am We. We, baby. Two by threes. Rotten bark fallin' off of trees. The circus in town with a horse act, in the center ring, that's dying. A clown smiled at me. I caught his wink and he ain't funny, see. See, baby. See and feel yourself. . . . Me. We ain't . . .

Free . . . yet . . . yet . . . or is there really a word called yet, or just a feeling yet felt? Like I ain't rich yet or I ain't free yet or I ain't gonna ever yet . . . yet. I ain't gon' never yet . . . yet. Yet . . . yet . . . yet . . . yet! YetYetYetYetYetYetYet-YetYet. . . . It was never ever nothin' that you done to me. How can I explain it? I can't explain it yet! 'Cause cellophane flowers don't need to be watered. They always the same, and Christ comin' again is still to come. *Yet* to come. Yet to come. And that's who you need, baby, Christ. You and Christ for you to come. For you to Yet. For you to experience, feel yet. Orgasm yet. Climax yet. Gut scream. Bust your rocks yet. He gotta come around you for you to come around with me.

And I just can't wait, baby, see . . . I just can't wait, baby, see. I just can't be cool and hang around any longer for the blond-eyed, blue-haired Christ to sound the word for you to come, 'cause every day I'm gettin' closer to yet without ever get. Do you understand? Without ever get . . . yet. [*sadly; change of thought*] The other morning I was goin' to work on the bus and . . .

[BUS SCENE. CHORUS *becomes people on an over-crowded bus. They begin acting out their lines.* CHORUS *members become bus driver, kid, cripple, drunk, old talkative woman.*]

CHORUS

[*jazzy chant*] Oooh—aaah. Ooh—aaaah. ooooooh. ooooooh. AH. AH! Ooh—ah. Ooh—ah. Ooh—ah. Ooh—Ooh—Ah. Ooh—ah. Ooh—ah. Ooh—ah. Ooh—Ooh—Ah. [*repeat*]

[*Different members of* CHORUS *say the following lines.*]

On this bus
    some dirt-face kid spat
    on this cripple woman's leg
Bus so crowded
    until the spit wouldn't
    reach the floor
  so it landed on her muscle part
                  and
  slid on down.
Cripple woman didn't say nothing.
She was too old to feel it.
Other people didn't say nothing.
They acted like they didn't see it.
Bus driver didn't say nothing.
He was smoking.

He couldn't fight that drunken man's arms.
So that's comfort in taking the transit bus
and leaving the driving to them and all that.
and incidentally the fare had gone up—fifteen cents.

BLACK MAN

And on the bus this old colored lady, she must've been a do-
mestic worker, was talkin' the ear out of this bus driver.

[*The* CHORUS's *talkative woman makes huge, exaggerated
physical gestures with her arms, hands, head, eyes. Her
voice gives out sighs and releases do's and da's and sobs
and wa's, throughout the* BLACK MAN's *talk.*]

I think he was Italian, or something or other, but this old lady
was talkin' the shit out of the bus driver. And you know what,
baby? I got to feeling sorry for that bus-driver sonofabitch.
Yeah, feeling sorry for the cat, 'cause in a way that is what
he deserved. Pity. [*louder*] Pity . . . pity, 'cause in a sense
he was the cause for it. The cause for that old black woman
talkin' his ears off. Makin' her think he was *even* God or
Jesus or Rock Hudson, even. I could choke. Hell, the old
bitch was trying to get her yets. Yet. [*laughs*] Trying to be an
integral . . . in–te–gral part of that bus . . . that world . . .
that heaven . . . with Jesus Christ driving the T6 to Takoma
Park. [*sadly*] . . . Yet, she got off like she was cool. But I could
see. I could see the hurt in her eyes. While all the while the
bus driver was cracking up inside thinking she was some ole silly
bitch. Some silly ole black bitch like them past-present roaches
who met their yets under my shoes.

[CHORUS *scrambles away like roaches.* BLACK MAN *stops one
member of the* CHORUS, *who becomes salesman.*]

Uh, salesman, would you hold up for a second? I've been waiting here to talk to you about—

[*Salesman turns to walk away.*]

Look here! [*fiery*] Don't walk away from me when I'm talking
to you. I said I been waitin' here to tell you about that mattress
and box spring you sold me six weeks ago and was never de-
livered. Why you didn't tell me the factory didn't have that
set? Did a goddam commission mean that much to you? . . .

CHORUS: *Salesman*

I don't lie.

BLACK MAN

What? You don't lie!

CHORUS: *Salesman*

I never lie.

BLACK MAN

You never lie?

CHORUS: *Salesman*

I don't lie. [*shows him sales slip*]

BLACK MAN

Bullshit, if you don't lie and don't get me no sales slip, 'cause
there ain't no nevermind between a written and a said word,
you understand?

CHORUS: *Salesman*

I never lie. [*walks away*]

BLACK MAN

I hope you vomit in your sleep and strangle to death . . .
dream-maker . . . myth-maker . . . money-makin' hip-shaker
. . . ha ha. Punk. Yet. Ha ha yet. [*new mood*] Yet I read the
papers, the *Times*, and I listen to the news on the radio, and
the only thing gettin' better is the commercials, it's been such
a long time since 1954. Commercials the only thing that done

89

got better, and they ain't nothin' to brag over. . . . Yet my son . . .

[*Member of* CHORUS *becomes son.*]

I kinda caught my son combing his natural hairstyle the other morning, and Jesus Christ the kid looked almost grown, and he ain't but fifteen.

CHORUS: *Son*

[*imitating* BLACK MAN] I said to myself—"Man, it's about over really, if you think about it, and even if you don't, you know. . . . [*pause. fast*] Across the street the people's dogs were barking like fire engines speeding to get paid Fridays. My radio played also in the background like next week's coming attraction down at the Republic. Kids was outside and below practicin' the "Popcorn Mother" without music. With just two fingers and a soul . . . groovin' as my son, my beautiful black man/son would say to me at the breakfast table. When he speaks? I don't prompt him none. . . . When he *does* speak . . . to me . . .

[*blackout on son*]

BLACK MAN

My hair just won't grow long anymore. It seems like all the breezes seem colder, chillier, more colder. Pavement seems harder, shoulders sloping forty-five percent farther down. It takes even longer to park the car or get some lovin'. Bright lights scare me. So do my dreams. So do my dreams make me kinda feel mad in the mornin'. My magic is going.

CHORUS

There's life! There's life! There's life on Mars and Venus.

[*Member of* CHORUS *becomes Muslim.*]

CHORUS: *Muslim*

[*selling papers*] Hey brother, there's life on Mars and Venus. Especially Mars, where there is true life. The true life. Can you beat that? Can you, brother, huh? The true life on Mars, million of miles from here. [*laughs*] Listen, you know all them UFO's people been reportin' about? They are really them folks from Mars checkin' us out. And check this out, brother, them little green men from Mars ain't really green at all but black. Yeah. Can you beat that, black. [*laughs*]

BLACK MAN

I bought the paper, baby. I bought the paper 'cause for once I believed them Muslims. Don't ask me why. Don't laugh at me, 'cause ain't nothin' funny.

[CHORUS, *hysterical laughter*]

Yet. For once I believed that cat, that ha-ha brother selling them papers on the corners. It was something about his eyes when he said it. I believe it. Mars. uh huh. Mars. Black people on Mars leading the true life. Free from, free from yets. And that night I prayed to Mars and I said,

[*praying. Female* CHORUS *voice hums blues tune during prayer.*]

Dear Mars . . . dear black brothers on Mars, please help us out down here in hell. Down here where we lead the lie life, and not the true life. The credit life. Pay next week until you die. Then die, nigger, die. Die, simpleton, die from heat exhaustion. Die from your own heated-up smell. Your own heated-up mind wondering what? Or who? Or how? Wonderin'.

CHORUS

Wonderin'.

91

BLACK MAN

Who to believe.

CHORUS

Who to believe.

BLACK MAN

What to believe.

CHORUS

What to believe.

BLACK MAN

Wonderin'. Wonderin'.

CHORUS

Wonderin'.

BLACK MAN

Wonderin'.

CHORUS

Wonderin'.

BLACK MAN

Who to believe.

CHORUS

Who.

BLACK MAN

What to believe.

CHORUS

What.

BLACK MAN

Wonderin'.

CHORUS

Wonderin'.

BLACK MAN

Yet. Yet. I believe.

CHORUS

I believe.

BLACK MAN

I believe our yet is in Mars.

CHORUS

Our yet is in Mars!

BLACK MAN

Our yet is in Mars. [*end of prayer*]
On Mars gettin' ready to explode in our brains . . . and mind.
Yeah, brains and mind, they ain't the same. One for destruction
and one's for construction. Our yet is on Mars. Our yet is yet
to come but our yet is to come and it's related to Mars and
Venus, too. The breeze is on our side. Animals, too. Grass.
Clouds. Sound. Liver. Beats. Thoughts. Hope. Faith. Charity.
Nature. Time. Time. Everything. 'Cause the man done messed
with everything and now he's up in outer space trying to mess
with our brothers. Our allies. Natural allies in outer space, and
that cat on the corner ain't even worried, 'cause he believes yet
is to come. To come without some Jesus playing rock music
and high on speed. Baby, a man got to follow his feelings, sometimes. At least one time. At least one time. That's why I bought
them daishiki shirts and them beads. 'Cause Junior's got a
point, though I ain't sure he knows why. Though that ain't the
point. He just does that all 'cause he got faith in hisself. Faith
in hisself. For once, faith in oneself. Hell, I ain't never been
in trouble. We make out O.K. Never been in trouble. My
mind's all right. You trust my decisions.

Act II

[Dance Sequence. BAND *is playing.* CHORUS *assembles on-*

stage dancing. During their dialogue a female member of CHORUS *scats—do–be—do–be—da–de–da–de–da.*]

CHORUS: *Member Number One*
The true life's on Mars and Mars is on our hearts, called rhythm anytime we hear the music. Space is the place. Black folks is the space race. The cosmic people who make up the space pace.

CHORUS: *Member Number Two*
The sun reflects our true names and enters our bodies called color. We can talk with our hands making congo drums scream with laughter or shudder with sorrow.

CHORUS: *Member Number Three*
Santa Claus is unkissed Sunkist compared to our shine. Shine, shine you looked so fine. [*sticks out behind*] Miss one stroke and your tail is mine.

CHORUS: *Member Number Four*
John Coltrane, the train—the locomotive man. Choo-choo-chooooooo. Blow de horn and breathe awhile. Lady Day singing blue holidays. Duke of Ellington—one-time man gigging at one-night stands creating his own cola across the land. . . . Wasn't nothin' ever fin–ah than Dinah . . . ah, Washington, that is.

BLACK MAN
Ever heard the water drop from a cool, clean, clear icicle, or was it a popcycle? Yeah, . . . yeaaaaah! Rhythm! Rhythm!

[*band plays* "I Can't Get No Satisfaction" *slowly.*]

I used to hear Junior talking about this guy, Otis Redding. You know, baby, like how good the guy is and all. Well, I remember this one day I read in the papers that this Otis guy dies in a plane crash. I don't know why . . . maybe 'cause of Junior or maybe 'cause I felt there was some kind of connection, some kind of bridge between me and the man, but I started listenin' to all his records. Soon I was buying the guy's records, they were so mean. I couldn't get enough of him and I kinda got to thinking to myself of all the niggers who never really got no recognition until they was dead. Like if me and all my friends would have listened to the man. Really listened to the man. Really listened to this Redding cat. Really sat down and listened to the cat singing "Try a Little Tenderness," maybe we might have tried a little soft touch. Maybe we might have laughed and slapped each other on the backs and gotten closer with each of our Juniors. Maybe by now we could of all been great. Or *Junior* would have thought we was great. 'Cause, 'cause the O—the big O—ain't . . . yet no Otis, ain't yet with rhythm . . . rhythm spirit. . . . His spirit is here and even Christ can't hang with that. All he can do is sit on "The Dock of the Bay" gettin' "No satisfaction." And yet . . . [*cries and laughs*] and yet . . .

[WIFE *is dozing.* BLACK MAN *looks at her curiously, then as if disgusted.*]

And yet I see my wife over there.

[*sound of drums.* BLACK MAN *chants his lament.*]

gone to sleep with a headache in her dreams and the world outside blizzing on by.

> And I know I'm mad
> And I know I'm glad
> And I know I'm sad
> And mad and sad and
>   glad/mad/sad
> All together

Blue lights shine from the sky and I don't know what to do. The curtain hangs, the garbage smells, the ants and roaches dance on the floor as my foot is numb and can't stamp them out. I see ebony statues, given to me last Christmas, laying on the floor dead, one arm broken and the white wood shining from within. I see the cellophane flowers blooming in the spring, the bugs, the fleas and ticks ignoring them. I see a clock radio vaguely behind the time and I wonder who am I and who was I and who am I will be, who am I and who was I and who am I will be. The morning comes. . . . The stars are shining and I know the morning comes. . . . A tongue is in my mouth, and I look at myself and scratch my balls and wonder, Is Peter Pan for real?. . . . Do I have to grow up and feel the hate of three hundred years upon my back? . . .

CHORUS: *Member Number One*

I see a broom in the corner, yellow broom straw, straw yellow broom. Fire ablaze . . . Fourteenth Street. Ablaze. . . . Neon signs on the ground, little black children reshaping their echo tubes to form freedom NOW.

CHORUS: *Member Number Two*

I see floors, floors. I see floors and florist and flowers being sent to mothers long lost and forgotten . . . to celebrate . . . long lost and long forgotten Mother's Day. . . . I see fathers smiling, patting their forlorn sons on the back for bringing about the dream.

CHORUS: *Member Number Three*

I see apartment buildings . . . silent at night with hope flowing out the window, thinking about eight o'clock in the morning, when the man shows his presence in the place which he rules by day, leaves by night.

CHORUS: *Member Number Four*

I see the green, yellow, red flag of Africa waving in my eyes, and I say to myself, I believe, I believe.

96

[*All sounds halt!*]

BLACK MAN

[*rising like a fiery black preacher—sermon*] I *believe* that [*emphasis*] you [*points to audience*] and me may be God in disguise. You and me *might be* God! in de skies [*points to sky*] rising every morning like the sunshine on my mother—my beautiful black mother nature . . . creating another black life motion from the motion ocean—motion in the ocean—leading to you and me, brothers. You and me might be God in de skies, yellow and om-mitting rayzuns in the sun shrivelled up small with the mind of a *Black Ton*. A ton, a black na-tion-ton. Twenty million strong and can't be wrong. Rampaging and raving up the biggest street in the north side of town and coming downtown to tell down stories to the mean man, fiend man, the mean-fiend man who sit downtown laughing at niggers uptown. Well, it's all over, because you and me just might be God, be God—eating fried chicken in disguise on the moon. . . . [*laughs*] Hear that, baby, eating fried chicken in disguise on the moon. Going around in costumes demanding trick or treat. Singing white-Christmas songs or collecting trading stamps for all your life. For all your goddamn life, without ever hearing any applause. Just for once I'd like to hear a loud voice coming from anywhere saying, "Man, I saw you" or "Man, I felt you, like man, I felt and saw you. Felt and saw you. You. You. You. For real, you actually—I ain't jiving—you as a you know.

[CHORUS *becomes workers in post office, sorting out mail.* BLACK MAN *sorts mail.*]

The other night, I got to thinkin' 'bout you and Junior, baby. Then I started thinkin' 'bout Momma and Dad and my brother Willie . . . my God, when was the last time I've talked to Willie? . . . And everybody in the apartment house and on the street and . . . and . . . [*freezes on his stool, reminiscing, forgetting about mail*]

[*member of* CHORUS *becomes supervisor.*]

CHORUS: *Supervisor*
Hey you, sort that mail.

[BLACK MAN *does not respond.*]

Sort that mail, remember that scheme.

CHORUS
Oooooooooooooooh. Aaaaaaaaaaaaaaaah. OOOOOOOOOOH. AAAAAAAH.

CHORUS: *Supervisor*
Remember that scheme, sort that mail.
[*yells*] What is the matter, you, are you ill or something?

BLACK MAN
[*shaken*] Am I ill or something? I have been working at this P.O. sorting out mail for nineteen ill-ass years, six thousand, seven hundred and fifty-five days, one hundred and twenty-four hours, that by dividing that tremendous total into eight-hour days with annual leave and sick leave—I can't stop and think for one moment. Not a second but a moment. Not *one* moment but *a* moment. There's a difference . . . yeah, just like in brain and mind.

CHORUS: *Supervisor*
[*interrupting him*] Pick up your check.

BLACK MAN
[*not paying the supervisor any attention*] One moment is a second in time while a moment is a moment of mine. A moment of my time. Not yours. Not the P.O.'s time but my time. My time.

98

CHORUS: *Supervisor*
Pick up your check, I said.

BLACK MAN
BOO! BOOOOOOOOOOOOOO!

[*Supervisor leaves,* BLACK MAN *continues with his moment.*]

My time. My moment. My moment to sit back a moment proudly and say to myself, "Roy Campanella is in the Hall Of Fame, Can't you hear the crowd applauding?"

[CHORUS *begins to applaud and build, as he does.*]

James Brown's Band is the best in the world. Can't you hear the crowd applauding?

CHORUS
Can't you hear the crowd applauding?

BLACK MAN
My son made all-city in his year in high school.

CHORUS
Can't you hear the crowd applauding?

BLACK MAN
Save up my money and got my wife a color TV.

CHORUS
[*louder, wilder*] Can't you hear the crowd applauding?

BLACK MAN
Applauding . . . applauding . . . yeah, yeah, yeah. Received telegram and roses congratulating me for makin' it so long.

CHORUS
Can't you hear the crowd appauding?

99

BLACK MAN

For . . . for being . . . appearing alive.

CHORUS

I wanna hear, I wanna hear, I wanna hear the crowd applauding.

BLACK MAN

Can't you hear the crowd applauding? You colored brothers on Mars come on down here and help us. You hear me now. Why don't yawl come on down here and help your brothers out? We need you, things ain't gettin' no better. I know you hear me talkin' to you. Prayin' to you. Wishin' to you. Treating you almost like some god and all. Don't pretend you don't know nobody, yawl! Why don't you . . . I say, why don't you hand out a big gold collection plate in the sky? Right over my apartment roof. I'll be out there. I'll see you. Got change, too, plenty of silver. Ain't been to church in years, been savin' up for you 'cause I can't be cool forever with my face out there in space. I know it's just a matter of time. A matter of a few more moments. A few more moments. My moments. Applaud.

[CHORUS *becomes active again*.]

Our moments. Applaud. His, our, moments. Applaud . . . together . . . applaud . . . together. . . . Yet the true life is on Mars. Baby, you woke? Yet is on the planet Mars.

WOMAN'S VOICE

[*off stage*] Junior? Junior, it's time to come in.

CHORUS and BLACKMAN

Aaaaaaaaaaaaaaaaaaaaaaaaaaaaaaaaaaaaaaaaaaaaah shucks, Ma.

WOMAN'S VOICE

Tell them you'll see them later.

100

BLACK MAN

We were just gettin' ready to go to Mars.

WOMAN'S VOICE

You can go tomorrow.

[CHORUS, WIFE, *and* BLACK MAN *begin taking off clothes.*]

WIFE

[*as small girl*] I wanna play playhouse tomorrow, don't like this game. [*exits*]

BLACK MAN

[*as small boy*] See yawl, tomorrow.

Lights dim out
End